The Ripening of Pinstripes

This Belongs To:
Mrs. Cocalis

The Ripening of Pinstripes

Rodney Torreson

Story Line Press
1998

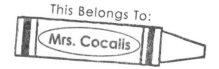

Published by Story Line Press, Inc., Three Oaks Farm,
Brownsville, OR 97327-9718

This publication was made possible thanks in part to the gener-
ous support of the Nicholas Roerich Museum, the Andrew W.
Mellon Foundation, and our individual contributors.

Cover illustration: Planet EARuTH by Mikhail Horowitz
Book design by Chiquita Babb

Library of Congress Cataloging-in-Publication Data

Torreson, Rodney, 1951–
        The ripening of pinstripes / Rodney Torreson.
        p.   cm.
        ISBN 1-885266-37-5
        1. New York Yankees (Baseball team)—Poetry. I. Title.
PS3570.0735R56 1997
811'.54—DC21   97-5650
                                                                  CIP

to Al Zyskowski

to Paulette, Tasha, Ted, and Travis

Special thanks to Russ Thorburn
and Herb Scott

Thanks also to Jim Allen, Linda Nemec Foster, Phil Hey,
Miriam Pederson, Jack Ridl, and John Woods, all
of whom helped and encouraged me through the years.

Acknowledgments

Grateful acknowledgement is made to the editors of the following publications where these poems first appeared:

Aethlon: "After a Season-Ending Injury to Key, You Ponder the Fragile Nature of Pitchers," "Entering the Lost Country of Dave Winfield," "Nobody's Fan," "Yogi, Though You're No One-Eyed Hunchback," "Your Streak's Generous Nature"; *The Age of Koestler:* "Roger Maris"; *Arete:* "Two Years Retired, Bobby Murcer Makes a Comeback Bid, 1985"; *Cape Rock:* "A Pitcher is a Beautiful Woman in an Old Movie"; *Contemporary Michigan Poetry:* "Don Larsen's Perfect World Series Game," "Dreams Should Not Dog Great Center Fielders"; *Elysian Fields Quarterly:* "At Penn Station the Team Boards the Yankee Special," "Because Dust Delivers Each Drop of Rain," "Billy Martin," "Maris and Dylan Came Scowling Out of Hibbing, Minnesota," "The Rivals," "To Comfort Catchers of the Knuckleball"; *Giants Play Well in the Drizzle:* "When the Babe Stormed New York"; *The Minneapolis Review of Baseball:* "Spring Plowing"; *The New York Quarterly:* "Jim Bouton, Unwriting"; *Passages North:* "Ryne Duren, Yankee Reliever"; *The Saturday Museum:* "Catcher and Son at Grossinger Hotel and Country Club"; *Spitball:* "Andy Stankiewicz, Yankee Rookie," "Gil McDougald, Yankee Infielder," "Joe DiMaggio Never Swings a Bat at Old Timers' Games," "Maris of the Cards," "Thurman Munson," "Tools of Contention," "The Yankees Bend to the Cool, Clear Water of Mirrors"; *Yarrow:* "1960, The Year Hook Hansen Owned the Cafe."

"Ryne Duren" and "Two Years Retired, Bobby Murcer Makes a Comeback Bid, 1985" also appeared in *Hummers, Knucklers, and Slow Curves,* an anthology of contemporary baseball poems edited by Don Johnson and published by University of Illinois Press in 1991.

"Ring Lardner Watches the Babe Take Batting Practice," was published in the conference proceedings of "Baseball and the Sultan of Swat," hosted by Hofstra University on April 27, 1995.

"The Rivals" was first published under the title "In Scattered Dodger Nests." Several other poems first appeared in different versions.

Contents

III

The Ripening of Pinstripes

Dreams Should Not Dog Great Center Fielders

who come in from the pasture.
Dreams should be pets gone fat.

In nightmares Mantle is
cramped, broad-shouldered,
in a taxi, hungry
as Mutt, his father,
who pitched his free time
to get Mick a ticket
from the mines.
He's late for the game, always.
      And DiMaggio at the airport,
despite his tall grace,
eyes darting like some terrier's
as he stands beside his luggage,
glances at his watch;
he is late, as if he's waited years
to board a flight
that takes him back
to Marilyn.

And Mantle's dreams
can't shake the guards.
The announcer says,
"Now batting... number 7,"
as Mantle finds a hole
in the fence
but can't squeeze through.
      And DiMaggio
for twenty-one years

sends six red roses
three times a week
to her Hollywood crypt
but they're a dog's
nervous patter.

The dreams of the greats should
be tame, trained
to open and close a gate,
with Mantle strolling
his heaven in center;
Monroe on her toes,
smiling, leaning into
The Clipper's arms,
returning the roses of her
red lips.

I

A Pitcher Is a Beautiful Woman in an Old Movie

for Yankee pitchers

not the dumb blonde but the one with finesse
who has good curves and fastball thinking
that's too quick to get around on,
who manipulates the leading man,
the director, the writer.
Her change-of-pace is like slipping
into something comfortable
as she sets the scene for the strikeout,
for her "get-lost-buddy," as men
go back to the bench.

She plays the field, one man for each
day of the week. They pound
their mitts, they leap, they dive
for ground balls, fall flat for her,
eat dust, play past their primes.

The pitcher, pampered when she makes the bigs,
is a young songstress in a movie,
her manager Frank Sinatra
who looks after the kid, who when
she messes with the opposition before the game,
warns: "I'm not going to send you flowers
when you're down in Toledo," or
"You butter up the hitters and they know
you're not going to throw at them."
These beautiful women on the mound,
who hurl such grace, who have delicate
careers, fragile strength, who feign weakness,
who batting could not hit their own weight.

When the Babe Stormed New York

the snows burned brighter.
Subways rose on a rail of wind.
They merged on some dizzy parallel
with elevated trains,
leaving trails of floss
as the two crisscrossed over city blocks
which the Babe blew past
in a cream-colored car,
banishing great Manhattan shadows,
while on his way to a Bronxville flat.
There he'd needle the Victrola,
nuzzle Flora's back,
as she giggled and squirmed
into the Babe's arms
from lonely outer reaches of her love seat.

When the Babe stormed New York,
he lit up every jittering nightclub.
They swelled and throbbed gloriously
the moment Babe, in a camel-hair coat,
stepped into the foyer.
It was God's blessing that the war was over.
The whole town smoked like those three cigars
Babe puffed at one time
in a show window of a cigar factory in Boston,
the Babe so big he throttled prohibition,
who died to his appetites every night
and in that forgiving hour before the game
was rubbed back to his body.

When the Babe stormed New York,
police began to believe in their nightsticks
like never before, and everyone was safe.
Babe left Flora behind at her door,
necking with the new fur
he bought her, while he'd go God-knows-where.
Babe waved a kiss
that didn't miss anybody, and the last
of those great firedogs sniffed
out the smoke of passion
as his nostrils flared,
and fans forgot they'd all be dead
in a hundred years.

Lou, Here's to Your Joyride to the Stadium

Here's to just marrying
and Eleanor's pyrotechnic eyes
out-sparking the motorcycle escort
rearing on back wheels
to flank your Ford.

Here's to the undaunted clearing of traffic,
to the outcropping of cars
rising again from the road's shoulders.

Here's to the striations
of burned rubber
giving themselves up
on this last day of the season.
And here's to the Mayor
who called your wedding to order,
and to New Rochelle's finest
ready to lop the tops
off stop signs
to keep your streak alive.

Here's to their pocket watches wound tight,
their puffed caps
friendly as a baker's.
Here's to the resplendent tipping of a brim.

Here's to "Hello there, Mr. Gehrig!"
and the quick tour
their eyes take of Eleanor,
as police hunch
by the rolled-down window.

8

Here's to your ardent eye on the road,
your bashful cheeks wet to the kiss
that's pure to your soul
as an oriole over there
on the fence post as the sirens blare,
and you motor past unblinking billboards.

Here's to teasing her
about pickling eels
and she thrusting out her tongue
to grow you one
beneath her wide, lazy hat.

Here's to the road
wielding you through its courses,
as cops toss tickets like confetti,
and telephone poles
lean in for love.

Here's to driving the swollen
middle of the road,
as all that hum
drums the underskin.

Here's to the pounding of pistons,
for running boards being urged on
until they are wings.

Here's to the branches of trees
undulating to
the swing of your hearts

like they do your
convergent arms before the mound.

Here's to trees
that will not fade
to the apostatic spades
of playing cards
that gamble on your fate
in a piece of sky
framed by yellow leaves.

Here's to you and Eleanor
driving into your life
in a day so bright
the sunlight heightens
to its own awareness.

Joe DiMaggio Never Swings a Bat at Old Timers' Games

The years lose their webbing.
The batters time their swings
to catch a baseball sleeping.
Old school boys who tried to
lace you into their shoes
wait for your name to swell again
in the P.A. system.

Yet at old timers' games
that end in three innings,
the score tied at pain,
they're glad you never bat,
bucking feebly against the gray
with some rocking chair swing.

They know you don't
give anything away
but keep your flourish
with a hand wave.

At night they dream
they can suck themselves in
without a word,
be inscrutable as zeroes
staring back from the scoreboard.

Don Larsen's Perfect World Series Game

Yankee Stadium, October 8, 1956

Despite the fall, Eden buzzed
in one crowded brain cell.
In this big fifth game against the Dodgers,
Larsen, whose best pitch was to the girls
at the bar, stepped toward the mound,
anxious to atone for his Brooklyn start,
hoping his mom in San Diego would watch
when he unwittingly heard God's warning:

"In the garden eat any fruit, but not
from the tree of evil and good."
Then he who broke curfew,
whose car once lost it at 5 AM
and wrapped around a telephone pole,
he who'd eaten from the wrong tree,
turned over control.

Though throngs circled him and teammates
smacked their gloves, God said,
"It isn't right for Don to be alone,"
and then put big Don Larsen to sleep
before the first pitch.
Then God reached into him for a rib
and formed a sweeping curve
to make his change of pace tail away.

And this was more than Larsen gave his wife
who filed this day to have his share
attached by the court, and with a snort
Larsen faced the mighty trees
of the Dodger bats, to avoid them like alimony.

For the Yanks Mantle homered, ran down
Hodges' drive. In mid game, perfection remiss,
Larsen felt pressure and a snake hissed
in every swing: "Larsen, give in.
Be the uneven pitcher you've always been."

How lovely and fresh a base hit would look.
And Larsen, nervous, toed the rubber
and felt it nub up in his legs till he
almost fell. But through the crowd
he heard the river of Eden roar.

And in the ninth, Furillo flied to the wall
in right, and Larsen gazed toward
the garden's edge, amazed at the leeway
within perfection, his pitches naked and unashamed,
and Campanella bounced to second.

Then Mitchell, the pinch hitter,
sidled up, sweet hits clustered on his bat,
and the serpent bobbed: "Eat the fruit
of the base hit. Impeccability God bears not
in anyone but himself.
Eat before the Lord intervenes."

"Help me out, Somebody," Larsen moaned,
and two strikes branded Berra's mitt.
Then Mitchell fouled one off the crowd's roar.

"Here goes nothing!" Larsen sighed
and God, lonely for perfection,

looked no deeper than Larsen's words.
"Nothing it is!" God's voice rolled
and no ball was thrown, though Mitchell
saw a fastball, outside and low,
and the umpire a third strike
and Berra a mystery hard and white,
and with a leap Berra landed
in Larsen's arms and the crowd cheered
and cheered for their own lives,
and headed out the garden gate,
everyone feeling perfectly fine.

1973, Buzzing Over Yankee Stadium

this man piloting a Cessna,
his proposal, "WILL YOU MARRY ME, BARBARA?"
trailing behind. Throughout his youth
the game had seemed colossal.
Once, seated in the stands,
he sensed, for a second,
something grand about to occur,
a thing inexplicably
beyond the realm of baseball,
as if opposing pitchers
would team up to retire Saigon and Da Nang.

Yet today from a plane, the game
looks smaller than he can bear.
Alou, Murcer, and White in the outfield—
dots of a broken line leading nowhere.

How trifling, then, must be his love,
for it concerns two people, maybe only one,
in a love too easily pinned to a ribbon,
plastic too orange, letters too blue,
as if even now
he must present his case
to Barbara, below, who is with another man.

When he flies over memorials
of Ruth and Gehrig,
he knows that in every love
there is stone
that protects the reaching one

or builds monuments like those
in deep center.

Onto the field,
unlocking the hard glare of security,
long blond legs raise over a rail.
Black flats drop down
like spring petals.

Barbara, near the pitcher's mound now,
waves a handbag,
blows a kiss that flits
a moment on everyone's lips,
as the crowd chants, "MARRY HIM, MARRY HIM,"
roused in favor
of a heart on a plastic banner,
trying now,
for all it's worth,
to rise above the plane's drone.

The Day I Meet Billy Martin

Tiger Stadium: September 19, 1986

In an aisle this colorman tries
to lose his face. "Billy," I shout,
"May I shake your hand?"—not knowing
his wife files suit this day
because he evicts her from their home,
or that he wears a lawsuit and tie,
his eyes distant when I say,
"You're the greatest, Billy. Billy,
you're the greatest!" "Thank you, Sir,"
and we shake and no time
to think this is his hand
and it's over like his
wife's grandmother's living in his house.
"Billy, you're the greatest!"—
his bony rage under his skin
stopped by the tourniquet of his tie,
who two days before said
if he were manager,
he'd can the coaching staff:
"White is useless. I don't trust Zimmer.
I wonder what side Torborg is on."

"Billy, you're the greatest,"
his mind elsewhere as if
he believes the two of us
could not be in one place. "Thank you,
Sir, thank you," and he turns
to take the long Yankee season
down the ramp; I bow

toward the rail where he catches
my hand. "You're the greatest, Billy!"—
as his black hair slicks back
toward his Yankee world.

Ending the One-Game Cataclysm

after Dent's home run in the
one-game play-off, Fenway Park, 1978

Yastrzemski pops to Nettles at third,
who all year made spinning dives
as if they'd lead to a time
when the dark or light
under the earth
meets him with a shout.

But this is no touted play
to break the barriers.

The New England geography stays the same,
except for the Boston Harbor,
bitten to chunks and never more bitter
than in this hour, leaving
the Sox to yearn for something deeper—
that Nettles left them to
damnation or peace
instead of threading that lonely feeling
that things will be better in the spring.

In the dugout a player
looks into his hands for a vein
that runs deep into the heart of all things.

Thurman Munson

Yankee Catcher: 1969-79

"Get me out of here," you said,
who missed your family,
felt separated as your shoulder
that seemed to go aching over the moon
in that last pennant run.

But the Yanks never
moved you closer to home—
Ohio, where garish
New York lights were soothed
in dew blades on your lawn,
who wouldn't let yourself
be grafted onto Reggie—
he of the inspired open wound,
who for the media
bled a team leadership never won.

Thurman, it was your time to go,
so you growled, "Get me out of here,"
raising the prospect of a trade
like that time, tired of fake jabs
and hammerlocks, you raised Cliff Johnson
over your head, hurled him fifteen feet.

All you wanted was a trade to your family,
play for Cleveland
at the bottom of the heap.
But New York even owned your father:
"Thurman belonged with the Yankees," he said.

Near the end
you preferred the stadiums deserted
where you'd stroll in street clothes,
sifting the powder of sky
for a road, a way to leave a ball club
in that hard chemistry of clouds.

And though you wrote the gospel of bad knees
we never knew you were mortal
until that off day you flew your Cessna
out of Chicago, and into Canton
where you peeled three trees
and flames thrust you into the lights
and you cried, "Get me out of here.
Get me out of here, please."

Rain Delay

for Rich
Metropolitan Stadium: August 26, 1979

In the box seats
the bright, laughing umbrellas are smug,
unaware their sheer number
disqualifies them as sages.

Yankee players are on the lip of the dugout
as if spoken there.

In one snort
the young bankers
add up the rain and leave.

Mickey Rivers shuffles to the water fountain, between sips
mutters to it
about a girl named Mona P.

Not knowing he retired
a Bemidji housewife searches through her program
for Harmon Killebrew.

Just fair—and inside the left foul pole—
two teenagers kiss rain
from each other's face.

Despite the updates from other games,
the scoreboard looks hopelessly introspective.

Billy Martin hollers across the field
to the Twins' Roy Smalley:

"Tell Calvin he's jakin' it!"
Smalley turns, smiles, taps his bat against his spikes.

In a white Concordia shirt a blond co-ed
prepares her Sunday school lesson
and wonders
if this game will be redeemed.

A freckled girl in a red jumpsuit tells her mother
she will count every seat in Section C, and does.

Under the grandstand
the bathroom lines have long, death-row faces.
In a man's front pocket
a transistor radio
is in the throes of its own small storm.

High in the rightfield stands
a Parkers Prairie farmer sees
bright, kernelled rows across the bleachers.

Goose Gossage, frowning through his Fu Manchu,
turns and snarls,
"We don't sign in the rain."

Out on the parking lot
in a bus chartered by a grain elevator:
revolving leather seats, knee-top tables,
decks of cards with rainy
bad-weather hearts.

The Yankees Bend to the Cool, Clear Water of Mirrors

"I go up and look at [my swing] in the mirror . . .
when there's a bad spell, I know where to get
the right answers."

Third baseman Mike Pagliarulo
The New York Times
July 27, 1986

In the old days mirrors were wild.
Mantle slid mirrors under doors in hotels
to catch flesh and fur.
And they were vain. Pepitone
blow-dried the game into his hair.

But Pags gains aplomb when pitches come
from his own reflected bat,
works on his stroke
until it's level as a cabinet mirror's,
his bat growing stalwart in glass,
the mirror's spark leaping onto flies,
flashing them out of the park.

Mattingly trains mirrors until
his bat smokes, fattens for each pitch,
his focus melting into the metal back
where he sees the Iron Man,
the mirror delirious as Dan Pasqua
begins to peer in.

The mirror, beyond mere reflection,
starts offering stunning visions of a stance.
In a week's time, since
the mirror is now in every room,

monster flicks take it from managing angles
to absorbing particles of the will
that dust the soul.

The mirror has the pennant fever;
it begins to hum, practice the "m" sound,
as if to bring great Yankees back:
Mantle, Maris, Munson, Murcer.

But no, the mirror, shiny as a tooth,
is talking to reporters.
They love its lustre, its photogenic glare,
the way it bites into the whole alphabet.

What the mirror wants is money,
it tells the media, more and more money—
a long term contract
carved into its darker side,
a Gilt Gesso Frame, molded swan-neck pediment
ending in acanthus whorls,
or the mirror will go mad;
it will hold its breath
until it turns black.

Pags calls it a baby
but the mirror screams, "Bastards,"
then laughs, shrinks the barrels
so the bats fit in their fists,
bounces Mattingly about the room,

slams Pasqua against a wall,
sucks them into its roiled waters,

then spills them out into the calm,
where the wood grows long again
and they laugh and swing
their slow, sweet bats
at bubbles of air, and the mirror
takes them into its watery arms
and they call it Mother.
They are calling it Mother.

1960, the Year Hook Hansen Owned the Cafe

he put in a counter with spinning stools,
ruled from the one by the register.
His apron, a foul angel,
looked after the food.
His butch bristled at the
penny kids after candy.

It was the year the Yanks lost
to the Pirates in the Series.
Afterward, Mantle wept;
the owners stalked Stengel
through wily, twinkling
woods of double-talk,
then forced him to retire.
Hook lost to the restaurant
across the street,
to Maude's pies and turnovers.

When the Yankees played,
Hook never let
any malted milks through.
In the Series he knew
that anything grinding
was sweet and fluffy
for the other team,
that when the malt mixer screamed,
the Pirates turned like a beater
through the bases.
He couldn't have been
less agreeable to anything

but the threshing machine
slicing fresh fingers.

In the 6th inning of the 7th game,
after Richardson singled
and Kubek walked,
Hook banged the table
for the talking to stop,
unplugged "Don't be Cruel,"
barricaded the door with the jukebox.

In one of the booths
a woman with white gloves
stopped searching for dust,
shrunk into her stand-up collar.
A salesman tipped his fedora,
then tried to escape through
the red and white checkers
of the tablecloth.

While Hook's fingertips
gripped a Lucky,
the barber sipped coffee,
peeked over the top of horn-rims,
dreamed of holding a sleek razor blade
against Hook's neck.

After Maris popped up,
Hook's long, mean cigarette ash
held onto that inning—

Mantle singling,
Berra taking time
to foul off a pitch,
then bashing one into the upper deck
before the ash dropped.

But in the ninth
it didn't help Terry
who gave up the winning homer
to Mazeroski
to have Hook slam
the drawer to the till,
upset to get
payment from a customer,
then promptly setting
the others down in order—
no coffee,
no phosphates,
nothing from the grill.

Roger Maris

In 1961, when J.F.K. brought his dazzling wife
to the White House and no one knew
his other need, and he'd fatherly kneel
by his daughter to wind them—to skip
Caroline through the Gallery for a photo
and toddle John upon lawn,
and the President was asking what we could do
for our country, Roger Maris did nothing,
thought many, while on his way to hitting
one home run for every year past 1900
as critics called him un-American for challenging
the memory of the man who shot alligators,
and said to Harding, "Hot as Hell, ain't it Prez?"
and fished with Lou Gehrig and smiled
from flashy cars, and went to the heart
of children's wards to give Yankee blood.

But Maris, "The Mad Bomber," rarely smiled,
spurned fans, wrote his hard look on their eyes,
hid in his apartment with Mickey Mantle
and old part-timer Bobby Cerv, and when
writers couldn't find him, they dug up
his mediocre years with Cleveland and Kansas City
and held them up to that Great Yankee Light.

And when the North Dakota boy stepped up
in his second at-bat of that final game,
his hair falling out from strain and him hating it,
and only his cap to keep him from being
a molting bird, his distant wife was in the stands,

her purse packed with letters that said he was lousy
and news clips fleshed out with glamour girls.

And Yankee Stadium held its breath like
the world at the Cuban Missile Crisis.
Fans choked back the cheers.
Concession men stopped barking hot dogs,
put off being the umpires of food,
as Maris, the son of a railroad man,
peered in for home run 61.

His hands resin, his swing the only sweet thing
about him, when Tracy Stallard, the Boston rookie,
wasted two pitches and boos crashed from
the upper deck, and Stallard smoothed the ball
to keep it from making the points of a star.

But Maris wished hard upon it, swinging,
and a star illumined its strange trajectory
into right, over the wall, and for one moment
none saw the Berlin Wall, and ninety miles
from the tip of Florida, Fidel Castro,
who loved the Yankees, tapped his cigar,
exhaling his black Havana smoke,
and for an instant loved America,
as Roger Maris knew it was gone, and
Mickey Mantle, from his hospital bed,
who had 54, knew it was gone
and Sal Durante, the young truck mechanic,
scrambled across the seats for a dream.

And Roger Maris, who said to *Look,* he could never
do this again and didn't, and also said
he "was all fogged out" as he circled the bases,
crossed home plate, knowing he'd never
be a Yankee, though his burly teammates
made a wall at the dugout
to make him bow, to crowd out his loneliness,
and Yogi Berra and big Moose Skowron
hoisted him upon their championship shoulders
and tried with their might to hold him up.

Tools of Contention

1961, Iowa

In winter I'd find Whitey Ford's curve
frozen into the hose
as if it were something Leaky found
and I'd gone deeper—past that period
when ball was stone.
That next summer the hose got cocky
when I turned the water on—
spun wildly, spat with the vigor
of a big leaguer.

Once, layers below what happens on a farm
I stood at the hose's end, holding it
like a whip, and cracked out a curve,
never letting go
so the pitch leaped back at me.
In Yankee Stadium Whitey felt
the Neanderthal in his arm.
On one occasion he's said
to have uncocked it—held it straight up
and let it bless the moon.

In the next layer Ford's sneaky fastball
which I'd throw head-on
toward the crouching hydrant.
Further down Arroyo's screwball
waddled in the rubber hose,
bobbed like a divining rod,
picking up the pitches in the ground.
When batters came to slake their thirst,
he'd rise from the bullpen.

All August I cheered for both
of my heroes and in the winter
carried their long frozen pitches
into the white clapboard house to warm,
with my finger traced their very backbones.

Nobody's Fan

Buck Paulson, you were big
back in junior high,
hunting Mantle
the way you searched out
kids in the locker room
and stuck their heads into toilets
or whipped them with wet towels,
sloughing wrappers
off penny cards
as if the ball players' guts
were sweet sticks of gum
that fell to the ground,
as if that was all
there was to glory.

But, Buck, you'd never know
how far Mantle
was from his card;
you couldn't touch him
though you stuffed our bodies
into lockers, rubbed our noses
against walls.

And though you'd headwrench
one of us, Buck,
at the end of some hall,
I want to say how far we were
from that place,

how far from our bodies
even before the mirror,
when we put ourselves
together with a comb.

We wouldn't know for years
what you had done.

II

1920, When Carl Mays Beans Ray Chapman

killing the popular shortstop
of the Tribe,
the dead man gets up and
with the help of two teammates walks
away from the batter's box.
When the irrepressible pitch
comes smoking down
Carl Mays' gun, buzzing "I love you,"
showing Ray Chapman a
thing or two about
getting by on that sickening thud
the fans heard in the bleachers,
repeating itself,
a mocking, transitory heart
so the dying lives on,
Ray Chapman shows how proper
we must be
even at the end
like the man in a restaurant
who chokes to death
with the utmost propriety.
Before Ray Chapman
folds over, senseless and dumb,
in the split second before
the ball blesses his temple
like a mother's kiss,
before he, always
uncanny on his feet
walks away dead, we like so
many very small gods

with our own pain
deep in our chests insist over
and over to the body quickly becoming
the stranger, "Not here, not now."

Ring Lardner Watches the Babe Take Batting Practice

(after the Black Sox scandal)

Oh how his flesh of plenty
sweetens the bones of our discontent!
This Babe of bluster and boom,
a plump fifth hot dog gobbling
his face, snatches my straw hat,
deposits it on Bob Shawkey's head,
then swaggers to the plate.
His friendly mug leans out toward
the pitcher: "Heat up the strike zone.
It's cold and shivering."
A pitch smokes and crackles inside—
his large butt barely back. Scowls,
wolfs down a sixth dog. Next pitch.
Bristles one over the
wall in right. "One for you, Ring.
Don't need to dress that one up."
His bald right thumb
pumps his belly. Back in the box—
bangs one that bakes the bleachers
in deep center, then slams one again
far past his own understanding,
way back, beautifully back, into
the envious hearts of angels.

At Penn Station the Team Boards the Yankee Special

Behind it the grinning steel
of the Iron City Flier, its companion train.
Inside them it is bright
as if all light were born there.

Outside, derbies and soft hats
float on a dour fog,
which seems to split at the blast
of a whistle, leaving a space
down the stairway for Gehrig,
who says, "Hi ya, kids,
I bet you fellahs are ballplayers."

From high in the concourse
brilliant wings of window light
broadcast the Yankee luggage
onto the street below. A train spotter,
pleasantly distracted, feels
the moment is ripe
for Ruth to appear. Lazzeri spits,
"Last I saw, he gave the eye
to some gal and she kep' it."

Extending out of his crouch,
catcher Bill Dickey halts,
arches his back—long suspenders flex,
this night smitten with heroes:
the gum chewing Benny Bengough,
Waite Hoyt and George Pipgras,
Wilcy Moore, then Cedric Durst.

And now the great Babe himself,
talking his moon face around,
brags he's gonna bang
a few down in Boston,
his size increased by half
as he gives himself away in autographs,

then onto the train,
claims a seat by the door, embarrasses Pennock
when he booms, "Piss, pass a cigar!"

while outside the train
a reporter in a bright bow tie
wonders how a thin green curtain
across his lower berth
can keep his belly laugh from
shaking loose his car, hurtling it skyward
at the mercy of the stars.

Give Praise for Bases

their stakes thrust boldly
into the heart of the park.
How they slay the hitter's beast,
yield a pathway to civility!

Take Murderer's Row.
Would Babe have been half as amiable
if there were no infield to circle,
no mirthful retraction of the blast
by his slack threading of the base line?
Would he of pipestem legs
have become a bird of horror?

And Lou, the Iron Man,
had he not administered the antidote
in that easy-to-swallow trot
after poisoning the ball,
how would he have followed up?

And the silent, stone-faced Meusel,
who acknowledged neither
fans nor press,
would he after clouting one,
with nowhere to run
have sprung toward a wall
with stammering feet, leaped
over it one errant time to kill?

Praise bases, too,
for spurning pride, pulling

the hitter from the box.
What if Lazzeri and Combs had digressed
to stand and watch a home run dress
in the holy robe of altitude?
Would they have turned
their anger inward—
if having sojourned, monk-like,
to the top of the Himalayas,
they found nothing more?

Give praise for bases:
inviolable, soothing bags of light
which bid a hitter
to set down his club—bags
which, when touched, alleviate
a batter's rage, iron him out
smooth, unruffled,
at peace with his god
as he crosses home plate.

Your Streak's Generous Nature

1941

How it keeps the foul lines crying,
the infield denying the brown
pasted flannel of old newsreel,
keeps the fences unforgiving,
at guard against memory loss
that crashes
against the wall to rob us.

Joe, even when the Tribe's Ken Keltner retreats
to deep third, ending your streak by
backhanding your drive,
it ascends, a limed base path beating
out of bounds, spiraling forward
to show us where we've been.

The clock, a turnstile, spins back until
grass clings to our legs, until
we open our smiling hot dogs
up and down the aisles,
and fedoras usher in
a lost breed of gentlemen.

Tombstones of box scores
overturn; then once again, Joe,
your hits host Tommy Henrich
and King Kong Keller
pounding the swelter of the afternoon,
around second Gordon and Rizzuto
floating like furniture;

George Selkirk, so many seasons
asleep in his skin,
leans amiably against a fence,
your hit streak singing
"Oh, Johnny, Oh,"
giving rookie Sturm
an endless career of one short year
that bled itself out in the war.

Oh for the phrasing of your bat—
how like Sinatra you swing
into each curvy pitch,
keeping each day
from going its own way,
my mother and father from never meeting
at the Hagedorn Cafe in Ruthven, Iowa
five years later,
two thousand miles away.

Your baggy uniform ripples in wind,
the nation cleansed in your swing,
as for a short time you hold back
the bat's slow flutter of leaves,
hold back the war,
keep the umpires from turning black
and perching at our door.

Andy Stankiewicz, Yankee Rookie

*"In New York the play of Yankee rookie Andy Stankiewicz
has been earning him comparisons to the late Billy Martin."*
Vern Ploegenhoef
The Grand Rapids Press

Hooray for the bright neon swing
of little Andy Stankiewicz,
for the sun-fringed scintillating fog
which never gave up on him—
though it had its doubts,
as it settled on him during tired bus routes
through two-bit towns.

Hooray for the Columbus Clippers, that fill-in bin
the Yankees reached in
when the top prospect sputtered.

Hooray for Andy Stankiewicz
spanking the ball to left field, now right,
who in this soft age
will take a ball to the woodshed.

Hooray for Stankiewicz never
becoming Stinkiewicz to the media
in the raw spring air
when the New York crowds are READY, READY.
Hooray for June 10, 1992,
when Andy is batting .323.
Hooray for singles pleased to be singles,
for his bat sweeping like a new broom.

Hooray for the reporter
spelling Stankiewicz right when coast to coast
days and nights are a mixed bag of pitches.

Hooray for Stankiewicz
stretching a single into a double in double time,
for manager Buck Showalter saying,
"There's nothing phony about him.
Everything you see is real."

Hooray for real 1950 baseball cards
sweating out the image of Stankiewicz,
for the hair-raising return of Brylcreem,
for the beautiful, buxom white foam of Burma Shave
and its tingling kisses before the mirror,
making a comeback for Andy Stankiewicz.

To Mattingly in the Shadow of His Ailing Back

Dark notes in the cheering now
as you slump through mid July,
then remind yourself
how your father's mailbag
never got lighter
nor his legs any younger
on that twelve-hour route back in Indiana.

For years, Don, you made
the base path the empty street
of a clean, small town.

You hit until you saw the lush lawns,
the spawning streams outside of town—
over a hill the foundry
beneath a dripping moon, all the young boys
not flexing before mirrors but fully grown,
heaving girders and melting iron.

Like in those days of Mantle
and DiMaggio before you
men in Iowa
bent on the step of their farmhouse
to uncuff their trousers
to let out oats and corn,
or in Montana, to shake coal dust
from their boots,
or they looked above the trees in New York
to unloose their eyes of concrete.

They saw you dive to the earth around first base
or in a crouch,
your feet planted at the plate,
and this, Don, is what got them to work,
as you weaved in your heart
the unsmirched mailroute of your father,
then thrived amidst the New York hysteria,
leading fans through the deep, rich woods of your bat.

Thirteen-Year-Old Girls and Handsome Kevin Maas

Before he drives the ball,
he crouches inside
the inside pitch,
sitting on a chair.

His big eyes and high cheekbones
make it dangerous
to young girls who leer,
falling hard for him,
who fall into his lap
from high in the third tier,
who for once
do not send out their skin
to sub for a bare and vulnerable heart,

who suddenly outgrow their New Kids' shirts
or feel dirty
in Madonna lacy bareness—
exposed midriff, desert of exposed back,
who modestly put on more clothes
before he swings,
staying with that face
to the depth of each dimple,

who will throw their Madonnas away,
raunchy Aerosmith, Twisted Sisters—
if they could
SOMEHOW get hitched
to this man, Kevin Maas,

whose middle name is Christian,
turn back that soft explosion inside them
when he turns on a pitch.

Billy Martin

Haggard but anchored by a scowl,
each time you do something routine
like jog to the mound
to check Guidry's signs,
the game not even on the line,
your bulging neck cords
score a game claimed
when you played second.

You straddle the plate
before your hit spins the Yanks
toward a pennant. Even there
you are somewhere else
as the kill steals from your eyes
and you're at the slaughterhouse
in the off-season, your bat, a maul,
as the cowhide across the plate
becomes cattle through the chute.

But even there you are somewhere else—
West Berkely, near your infidel father.
As you raise the maul,
your mother takes her stance
with a hand-mirror, to crash
each window in his shiny new car.

At the Copa,
before the Yanks trade you,
when you punch a man

to the cloakroom floor,
you admit being somewhere else.

And even when you do something routine,
when your spikes claw the mound
to cover your dreams,
you are somewhere else.
When you nod your pitcher
toward the shower,
you lunge where the fly
blows back toward home plate
to rob the Dodgers. But even there
a darker ball begins to unwind.

And each time you do something routine
like trot back to the bench,
tension traps under your skin.
And even as you crouch in the dugout
you are somewhere else
as your team plays through
the pain in your life
until your players
don't know who they are
and even Goose Gossage
wants out of New York,

and though you win, you have to
triumph again the next moment
in hundreds of games played

between every game
until they fire you and
you wear dark glasses
before the press,
to cover up
the places you've been.

Ryne Duren, Yankee Reliever

As a nation sleeping under Ike
worshipped its image in the TV,
the real mirror was the
groggy one in your goggles—
something frightening returning
as a glare, as you swilled
your way toward the strike zone,
throwing at shoulders to find
the plate, practice pitches
crashing on the screen.

Rockwell's brushstroke
refused to wander;
the world never appeared so round.
In you we glimpsed
it was flat after all
with places for falling.

For years the hitters slumbered,
their bats wilting in the sun.
Oh Ryne, how Ike's closed stances
positioned their feet
until your drunk fastballs
made them arch their backs and dance,
buzzing them alive when they'd count
their bodies in a flinch.

Before you fell into disfavor
and Kennedy was sworn in
and atom monsters swallowed up

a part of the sea—
once, before that,
when Ike was wearing
his white, white shoes
through the dark hallways of America,
you hurled a ball
which the eyes of the batter,
catcher, and umpire missed,
as if it were the 1950's
lost inside shadows—
a whole decade nobody saw.

Catcher and Son at Grossinger Hotel and Country Club

(circa late 1950's)

The flurries against the hotel
the same tweed
as his overcoat,
Elston Howard crouches
in the snow,
grins at a cap and earflaps—
his small son.

Chin music turns sweet
in his upturned hand,
who will lift
a drooping head, catch his son
up in his arms

and each home run,
each pitch wound forever
in that clock,
his catcher's mitt.

The Rivals

In scattered Dodger nests
these fledglings sit:
Preacher Rowe, hair pin-feather thin—
graying even as the credits wane.

Joe Black and Clem Labine
close eyes to read the heart's
own sacred scroll,
open mouths while hoping to be fed
dangling foul lines
or an outfield wall.

Duke Snider wishes
he could swoop down
on those dead balls
that dropped before his glove,
on that blooped one-liner—
"What if he'd done more?"

Carl Erskine chirps
toward the twirled vibrato of his curve,
the hooted strike-out call
from the owlish umpire
growing small.

The voice of Campanella flutters wings
above his wheelchair's metal nest.
Furillo, ruffled,
wary of a fall,
whose winged feet
left no field so vulnerable.

Pee Wee Reese
pecks at those Yankees even now,
and at the happy,
gutless ones who would devour
those peerless years as mash—
something bland and grainy,
void of fire.

Here's for those men
who would piece things back
to Brooklyn once again.

Gone are their insulated days
within the shell of Ebbets Field,
apart from our frailties, mortal ways,
when with the yoke
of nourishment, the sun,
they were inextricably bound
before retirement pecked its hole.

And where are Robinson and Hodges
and Billy Cox? How about
that storm that pushes hard
against our chest
when we feel most threatened
and easiest to take?

Lord, for that terrible worm
of this, our world,
fed to these ones to make them beautiful—
more so than when they played.

Gil McDougald, Yankee Infielder

*"The event which, in most people's minds, brought the turnabout
in [pitcher Herb] Score's fortunes came on the 12th pitch of a spring
night in 1957 at Cleveland Stadium. Gil McDougald laced a 2-2 pitch
straight into Score's right eye."*

Sports Illustrated
August 7, 1961

Your luck too, religious boy.
Your batting eye offending you,
you plucked it out,
not hitting up the middle.
Better than your body
burning forever in Score's eye
where hell was born.

In the blistered rods and cones
of his retina, you descended,
after third baseman Al Smith
grabbed the glance
and threw to first,
Score crumpling, the eyeball hanging
from its frayed mitt.

They shifted him off
on a stretcher, and when
Doc Kelly opened the lids,
your unformed image
burned in the membrane,
your bat too, inside of Score's eye,
his tongue checking bridgework,
then mumbling, "Mac,
it wasn't your fault,"

as if Score had a vault
of gold pitches, this flame thrower,
who couldn't move his head,
who'd pitch his hand
against a hospital wall,
his mouth hot and dry
for a miracle.

His own mother bent your ear:
"You have no control
over where you hit the ball."
But you began pulling
everything right,
trying to change
the constellations,
your average falling
while you writhed
in Score's eye.

You said Herb was
a helluva guy
and meant every word
as the two of you burned
strange offerings
to the Lord.

In the Series' Sixth Game, Reggie Courts the Moon
(October 17, 1977)

> *"Reggie Jackson belts three consecutive homers and thrills a*
> *crowd of 56,407 at Yankee Stadium as the Yankees win the*
> *Series in six games."*
>
> Day by Day in New York Yankee History

1

Across his chest
Reggie felt a ripening of pinstripes.
In batting practice
his dominion stretched to every pitch.
Though his hits did not break
the layer of ozone—to invite
a harsh reprisal from the sun—
they got the moon's attention,
which beamed on him
like a portrait's wet, eternal eye
that follows one about.

Far below her,
Reggie vowed to be the man in the moon.
He knew that deep below her surface
the moon was sap.
Before the harvest
in east-side saloons,
he never felt such a tremble.

Already, the Yankee-Dodger match-up magnified
beyond the swollen bags of Lasorda's eyes
as he scoured for Dodger blue
in this wrong sky,

beyond Cosell's need
to lead each mere at-bat
into some black hole of study.

For the moon, meanwhile,
two hundred thousand miles of eye strain
was getting to her.
And she tired of inspiring,
waxing for the sum of her yawn,
hovering too high above the lovers
to be sure what went on.

Still, she had the uncanny eye to catch
any rooster's head before the hatchet,
or dead and swollen cow
who looked ready to fly up
and over her, any deer
blown to bits by barbed wire.

And she was beautiful.
Earth girls swooning before her glow
and with no lunar standards
believed as such—even as they
reached for makeup
for their own mugs
and urged on their own
moon shapes in the mirror.

The moon intercepted radio waves
as Reggie stepped

into the box
in the fourth and fifth,
his biceps able to wreak such havoc
that fans saw them
flex a second time in his neck.
In each of those innings,
he stung a home run on the maiden pitch.

2

In the eighth the moon cried,
"Imagine unleashing
three impoverished comets
for goosey home runs.
Some celestial thrill!—
and these comets owning
neither head nor tail."

What did then arouse her
were strums of warm air
stirred up by applause;
curious indeed, she lowered herself
in goddess form
over the stadium.

With Reggie at bat
before the third home run,
fans could feel a nation of farmers
turning the seasons

there in his arms:
combines gathering South Dakota wheat
in huge yellow sheets;
Michigan apples bobbing
on a bough of wind;
and moonward now, a garland of
enameled corn
ascending in Iowa elevators.

In recent years
rumors own that the few fans
not glued to Reggie's moves
saw her primping
above the Goodyear blimp.
"Oh how her moonbeams
filled high heels,"
they confess to the unblinking tabloids.

Only those fans
caught what happened next:
The instant he cracked
Charlie Hough's first pitch,
the blast went for her breast
in a circuitous course,
since it first sailed
nearly five-hundred feet toward deep
center, its black, empty seats.

She, skirting the ground,
gaining the awed perspective of a human,

dropped down upon him
with all the burden of a plume, and
in her best understanding
of what lovers had done,
rode him piggyback around the bases.

He called himself a good man,
felt against his back
two moon parts shimmering,
her tanktop knocking out a rhythm
in jogging-time.

They didn't get past first
before she worried
that she would lose him.
How it burdened her to know
that her loony, airless atmosphere
had made many stars disappear—
Reggie, such a resplendent one,
that the Dodger first baseman
secretly clapped in his mitt.

She then began tossing moondust around,
not for sport or love of the crowd
but to rid herself of this
blemish in her nature.

She cast off her madness
in a few smooth, powdery puffs
which she blew from her hand,
but the dust turned to a devil,

which a half-inning later
led thousands of fans
to charge onto the field upon the last out,
leap beyond the shadows of policemen,
beat each other's heads in
where something the least
objectionable stuck out,
fans frothing after bases and turf,
ripping out seats,
flinging them for
all they were worth
as if they'd transform
into the crudest wings.

Reggie, in right,
with the moon at his side
dodged and elbowed the fans,
escaping toward his
underworld beneath the stands.
But the moon
buried her lips into Reggie:
only by that kiss
did the moon hold on.

3

In the clubhouse
champagne married them.
The moon prepared herself,

rolled back up,
a cool but fiery circle,
bowled through Manhattan,
then over country roads,
past corn bins and silos of dairy farms,
blessing the pumpkins
she'd once given evil grins.

Beside herself with pleasure,
she rolled over an orchard
for the sweet perfume of cider.

She loved the grass stains
on her legs as she named her body parts
like the naming of animals,
and loved, as well, her mulchy smell.

After Reggie appeared
in the great white suit of his Cadillac
and slipped from it at the gate
so his heart could be pure,
he noted that her scent was of the earth.
This, he took as
the highest compliment.

Then every fence wobbled with delight
for miles around.
The beaks of passing birds
made happy hieroglyphics
as he went into her

and the soil stirred
toward a new richness.

In his hands
Reggie felt her tailspin toward morning
and trees sacrificed themselves
by self-induced lightning
in a nearby grove.

Because Dust Delivers Each Drop of Rain

Billy knows
there's a point in Ricky's steal
where dust stops
and water begins—
not during the sprint
when the sky tugs on his limbs
but before the ump's arms
scissor a safe cloud
and Ricky emerges in one fluid burst
to dust himself off—
during the stony headfirst dive,
when Billy Martin,
knowing all things—
and having made a line
to the cooler—sips Ricky's
cold headfirst slide.

To Comfort Catchers of the Knuckleball

for Butch Wynegar

Yes, there's a moment before the knuckler
when the batter and catcher
are on the same side,
the strike zone between them
like that river in *The Red Badge of Courage*
before Audie Murphy runs.

In the woods that first night
he talks across the water to a Reb
and they realize they're both
boys before the knuckler,
that neither of them invented this pitch,
when boasting in the dugout
seems years behind,
and the mind itself floats and twists.

Jim Bouton: Unwriting

*"You've done the game a great disservice. . .
What can you be thinking of?"*

Commissioner Bowie Kuhn

The gall it took
to drill that peephole you called *Ball Four*
like those that players bore
into hotel rooms,
when they zoomed in
on the secret lives of skin.

You wrote about the Mick
shoving kids aside, pushing
through them like turnstiles;
Maris flicking off the fans
in Tiger Stadium; in my dark dreams
I was one of them.

Yet I sensed
that the stars were human
long before you wagged your tales.
Your cap flying off,
you'd stoop to the level
of a laborer, the cap a great leveler,
even as you won twenty.

You never out-hurled sweat,
even when your fastball,
the best Mantle ever saw,
was the high priest
that annulled the marriage
between bat and ball,

74

your cap never sealing
in an era when Yankee heads—
after the strike-out pitch—
produced a pleasing blip
in sync with Mason lids, as the ball
burned its way around the horn.

And if your thoughts ran bitter
after your sore arm
as your teammates said,
that would not have been surprising
to a kid who saw
your cap falling,

falling until
I could not be further deceived
by uniforms that were sleeveless
in the snowy field of a TV screen,
not believe the players
mouthed mothballs between games,
that street clothes
were a strange bacteria
that would have killed.

But lately I note
how you survived
for a second lifetime
eight long years after being released,
how crossbones and skull
stamped your knuckleball,

despite the Dodgers' ridicule
as they gnashed
and struck out.

When I think about you
inventing vanity baseball cards—
four perfect corners
adorning even the most insufferable
bench warmers moving slow—
creating Big League Chew,
where gum bubbles mimic
a sweet breathed world
we knew long ago,

I know that you are unwriting
Ball Four, unwittingly
restoring each myth,
even now as you pitch, at 51,
for the Little Ferry Giants, semi-pros.

Now Mantle, too, grows
into the gee whiz sort
he portrayed on *Home Run Derby*
thirty years before,
no longer sullen
but at ease during shows, his head
floating among memorabilia.

And your old fastball
I see again, even briefer than before,

so that in one cosmotellarian leap
there is no space
between the mound and the plate:
your mitt and the catcher's
one and the same.

Though your buzzing butch
still stings the memory,
your cap falling off
no longer signals that by game's end
the Yankees are flying from
between their buttons,
brushing by their fans—you unwriting
so that behind their pinstripes,
those taut, blue bars,
the Yankee greats,
though they be tortured
are again model prisoners.

Sometimes the Yankees Love Us Back

like once when
a drunk
twenty years older,
a hundred pounds bigger
than my brother
and seated behind him
behind third
at old Comiskey didn't
like his white hair,
taunted him, shoved
knees into his back,
was holding them
there when Don
Baylor drilled
a foul, which Rich at
the last second saw,
then snapped his head
left, so the ball
exploded upon
the forehead of the lout,
who, suddenly polite,
hung on
until the fourth
when his dim bulb
dimmer, his
buddies' arms under
each shoulder, this
newborn big-
hearted soul staggered

out onto
the down ramp, taking
all the world's
pain with him.

III

In the Midst of a Long Baseball Strike, Gil McDougald's Deafness Is Lifted from Him

After twenty years his hearing paints
this earth again
the way a blind stretch
of an arm brings to life surfaces,
shapes, in the far
reach of a basement.

Oh, the sounds his hearing
will brush against, like the heartbeat
striking us, keeping us conscious,
when wood and ball break down
in the body.

In his garage his voice,
that stranger, hammers and misses
the nails of pale words—
noises everywhere but in his head,
where the hits of replacement players
fall planets away from him.

Lord, there's no song
in Yankee bats, the sweet crack,
that opening of a vision.
Instead he leans into his lawn
late at night
to hear worms like roaring water
through their holes,
as they overhaul baseball's stinking carcass,
or, choking his bat

to reflect his old stance,
the left foot pointed at the
pitcher, his bat held high and
back, Gil hears it cry like a lonely rib
in the body of the first man.

Mickey, Once Our Days Made Their Face in You

Even after
they carried you off
on a stretcher
in the '51 Series,
when your cleats
caught on
a drain cover—or
was it falling stars
striking your knees
that slowed you?—
you persevered
to trick the distance.

Our expectation, untethered,
preceded you through
the TV age.
In living rooms
before the flurried screen,
our enthrallment with
anything that moved
on the wane,
we awaited your image
in the snow.

Sometimes, pressed beyond
our knowing, we lifted
your swing
above the citadel
to practitioner,
healer of the soul,

while you, on deck,
fitted your helmet.

Even that blast
off Stobbs of the Senators,
we waited for
beyond the roof facade
from which it bounded,
you, the sacred
ghost, invisible arrow,
digiting more
than 600 feet,
then floating through us.

Still, if you swung
big, we swung bigger,
to meet you in the shadow
of our need.
And there, after you retired,

and we turned to
the wife, the kids,
the falling through
of the word "father,"
the emptiness at the
bottom of prayers,
the parietal blunting
of our dream speed,

it was you that beer
began to swill,
the distance of home runs
slipping down like
a folding rule,
until that day last winter,
your liver killing
you to the certainty,
you entered
the Betty Ford Center.

There, with outstretched
heart, after
all these years,
you, mortal now,
wizened father of
the son you once were,
wait for us, where we fans
are blessed,
where they take your
pinstripes at the door,
the blue veins feeding
us in secret.

Paul O'Neill, Descendant of Mark Twain, Starts Us Down the Wide River

With that whimsical lift of his right foot
when he spins that big wheel, his bat,
it's so clear you're surprised
you never noticed before
how Tom and Huck's spirit
throws real style
into his stance.

You make out his lofted steamboat
on a watery seam,
as whistle blasts cast out
the smoky shadows of gulls
and Tom and Huck, small and smaller now,
on the starboard side, motion to us.

Before you know it,
you join them upstream over
the jagged rock of the stadium,
toward the Midwest,
then down the Mississippi,
over the Sawyer fence and each wall
our Aunt Pollys had us whitewash.
Over every barrier
until, Black Avengers,
we dock on that verdant
unspent island
of our own at-bat! Oh, for peace pipes
snapped on our knees,
for glorious wars against walls,

for forcing back a bald-eyed pirate,
pocked proxy of a foe,
then taking on, with a club
smote from a dead oak,
five daggers of an unleashed star.

After a Season-Ending Injury to Key,
You Ponder the Fragile Nature of Pitchers

knowing that Yankee arms,
like the others,
are doomed salmon climbing the windup,
or a walleye's spiny
imbuement of the pitch,
these fish out of water,
their gills gasping
in an opening and closing fist.

The hurlers at the mercy of fish arms,
which still have something left,
whiplashed as they are,
even as they expire
on a stringer of human bones,
cold-blooded, remembering when
they were hooked into being
golden arms, in a sun-bleached pond
in some boy's childhood,
now impressing upon a sphere
its slippery motions
which nibble the strike zone.

Fortunately for pitchers
fish can take years to die
in the brutal air, revived
again and again the last instant
in ice bucket or whirlpool.

A live arm winning the Cy Young
might be the next fish laid bare
on the table, the pitcher's guts removed,
as if to prove
he was merely a sidekick all along,
the fish slipping off of its breath
when needed most,
leaving, say, a David Cone, alone,
as if being well-spoken
gets anyone out, or the fish ripples
flatten, crushed floatingly by
forests, spindly trees, through which
fish were meant never to fly.

Maris and Dylan Came Scowling
Out of Hibbing, Minnesota

This town boasts the world's largest hole
and it bore through both of them.
Each had what the other did not:
traits stuffed, overgrown,
as if in the forty years that Hibbing moved south
and the Hull-Rust pit encroached,
things got mixed up: scent of dogs, mail routes;
gene pools split on couch, banister, and branch,
entering leaf buds
and x and y fell from the alphabet
or scored in throng.

Maris born for Pat Boone shoes
but no Pat smile, shoulders of the Mesabi Range,
while Dylan was born
in Hibbing at age six,
for leather jacket and boots,
and ducktail, no shoulders, but a shrug.
One turned toward bang, one hum.
And at Tiger Stadium,
before Maris hit his fifty-eighth home run,
he leaned against his bat
and watched Canadian geese,
one large flock fly over;
it was the melting down of Stone Age man;
it was the sixties being born.

Dylan, born when his old self moved in from Duluth,
likely made concoctions in the pit

as boys are apt to do
wherever a fence's law breaks down.
When cells dislodged
as old Hibbing was overturned,
they came alive in contact with his skin
and each fish mouth nibbled a way in.

When Maris had looked up,
something deeper than home runs
held him like the white band does
across the goose's throat.
He squinted at the v-shape,
he who hated travel
from Kansas City to New York,
who made this leap because of Dylan
(Dylan's leaps were good for two)
who was nurtured in this soil
where houses, churches, saloons and stores
leaped each other for those forty years.

Maris stood outside the batter's box,
put off the cunning in this world,
put off the frowning Terry Fox, and Dylan wailed,
"I leap to Selma and Vietnam,
I leap into the veins of leaves,
I leap into chlorophyll,
I leap into the mountain goat's horns
and turn them upside down."

Then Maris saw Hibbing as a shell-shocked town,
the courthouse crumbling, its windows blown.
And before he stepped in and hit the ball
into the upper deck in right,
just below where the geese had flown,
he glimpsed Dylan's myopic vision,
everything from Saigon to Hibbing
blurred into one,
and Maris leaped over gender
to a place where Dylan
raised ore dust in his throat and sang
and Maris tempered his distrust of the fans
in a place just the other side of music.

Spring Plowing, 1965

"This is the big leagues. We don't have no plowed fields for you to run through."

Casey Stengel

The *Game of the Week* calls
but the farm boy plows
for corn and beans.
The Yankees, in their decline,
take the field.

If the farm boy could put
himself in each swing,
he'd save their season.

Instead, he throttles
a tractor through dust,
sees Pepitone
doff his cap, his wig
askew, hide his head
in a teammate's armpit.

Tresh hits a dirt clod.
His home run is dust.
Mantle limps out a bunt.
The ruts jar his bad legs
toward retirement.

If the boy could hold his breath
before the balls and strikes,
the Yankees would win
and the boy win the girl
in the dark. But Maris grounds out.

His ball has no eyes
to find the furrow
through the infield,

as the boy tills
his team under
and pimples break out,
his voice crackling
among the ruins.

Maris of the Cards

At thirty-three, singles lined his forehead;
his sore hand shunned the handshake
at the start of the swing.

It was fitting that his bat,
torrid in the frenetic New York pulse,
slowed to a country road outside St. Louis.
Yet for two years his single would flush
Brock and Flood from bushes,
keep them flying—
even when a pitcher shaved them close.

That's all Gussie traded for,
this handler of pitches who Clete Boyer said
could hit the slowest dribbler to third
to get a run home,
plus swift feet and a strong intersecting arm
that could cut a base line,
make home plate an island,
Gussie knowing he was leaving
the great power hitter behind
in the shadow of Ruth.

Perhaps his swing declined
toward homemade fenceposts
that made their way across Missouri
and inclement weather in old bones.

His singles mingled with the everyday,
he talking one to a reporter,

then walking it back to his motel,
no loud mob to rob him of his footsteps
after home runs harried him.

All those power numbers
shorted out in those final New York years,
void of romance,
were ground now to singles, sac flies, and bunts,
as he helped the Cards to two flags
and his swing slung the hash of happenstance.

Entering the Lost Country of Dave Winfield

The sun, oppressive
as a rest stop view
of the interstate,
burns red above the collar line
until our bodies grow weak
and we forget the nine-to-five.

For a moment we glimpse
the tribal and quick:
a dozen men
stretch their bows
and climb in, disappear
into their arrows,
split bare the time-bound fabric.

Only then
far down the aisle
do we try on Winfield:
a toe touch here,
shoulder swivel there,
the earth rotating
in his neck roll.
Winfield, between pitches,
tugs at his pants,
adjusts his high hips to the fan,
while the paint beneath his eyes
seizes the body
and his heart drum harnesses
the unraveled beat
of factory smoke.

At the swing
we lope over centuries of flying ground
with his long, leggy
beautiful gait

to snare the ball
the second before it is eclipsed
by a condor, where

small winds whisper what they know
in a place where the moon
hangs so low
it could eat a leaf.

The Fans Versus Ed Whitson

"[His] career with the Yankees... marked by poor pitching performances, constant jeering by fans and reported threats to his life—finally ended today..."

The New York Times
July 9, 1986

Their world in his hand
made their car break down,
the kids need braces, the wife drop
their house keys into a hat.

They would chase his van, rod it
through a red light,
pound nails into his drive,
would have burned his house,
killed his family.

Maybe the mounds are high
because there are pitchers under them—
victims of fans
who can charm no ball
nor fool anyone: themselves,
their children, any great blind face.

Two Years Retired, Bobby Murcer
Makes a Comeback Bid, 1985

"The life of a soul on earth lasts longer than his departure."
                    Outfielder Murcer
                    quoting philosopher-poet Angelo Patri
                    at Thurman Munson's funeral, 1979

After your ascent into the
broadcast booth, then higher
into the rites
of the front office,
your soul still roams the field,
combs it for hits
that never got through.
Your ear cocks
for that song: the body
raining hard on the base path.

In Florida, when you pick up a bat,
the deep woods stir.
A practice swing and the river
jumps into your wrists.
You make good contact
with that world
you've seen from the moon.
As if the Yankees remember
your words: "A man lives on
in the life of others,"
they hand you a miracle; you sign.

What is lonely as one hit
in twelve at-bats?
Call it a rain dance

in the season of old bones,
your playing four games
while the trees grow back,
your fist, stone,
as you dream back your speed,
run faster than you can run.

A Boy Is Knocking

at Babe's door
on the third floor of
a hotel that is back, back,
and outa here. It is Babe's wooden unpublic
vertebrae he knocks on, a winding
stairwell around from any place the
boy has been.

In his shoes he feels the
creaking of wood under
someone's feet. His rapping makes
the only other sound in his world.
Though he doesn't know it, his knocks
awaken the old varnish of
a summer night, keep a bellhop
on a busy floor beneath him needling
and bobbing with his tray.

He is an ordinary boy who's always
played best through other
shoulders. Still, he keeps
knocking at the keyhole
for a full opening, for a burly bathrobe
draping a great gargoyle
who suddenly appears. A spew
of cigar smoke, a wink from the Babe
and the boy has slipped

out of his head,
his spirit now wheeling from
the ceiling toward the slick light
of Babe's black, shiny hair.

The Called Shot Home Run

Wrigley Field, 3rd Game, 1932 World Series

The Cubs leading by a sneer,
Babe wagged a finger
at each thorny strike,
pointed toward center
when it didn't matter,
since the archetype of Babe's pointing paw
was revealed in Zurich
by Jung a season later.

Floppy-eared Guy Bush
taunted from the bench,
as a bad year burned in the Babe,
who was bragging and fat.
When Babe flung the tree,
he thumped the ball into
the stunned center field bleachers,
growled "Meathead"
as he circled the bases.

On the bench, Herb Pennock,
the great lefty, said
"Suppose you missed.
You would have looked
like an awful bum."
And Babe at the water fountain
rolled his head
like a great stone
and laughed,

this Babe of Babes,
who later said

106

he hit the ball up
and "Zowie, the wind
did the rest,"
who always got
the swing of the crowd,
not the one in Chicago
whose game turned sour
at the Babe's feet,
but that other crowd
which floats among us
breathing forever and ever
into box scores.

Yogi, Though You're No One-Eyed Hunchback

At the plate sometimes, your pendulum, a club,
you'd fight off bad pitches
to win the life, the sky-blue love
of a beautiful gypsy,
whose name ruled the graffiti walls
of a New York subway.

At night, high in the bat's bell tower,
where cheers still ring,
you'd draw her into dark corridors
that Steinbrenner never explored
to hold her close
and wrap your pain in her long brown hair.

Slowly you would share those times
when, the Yanks on the field,
you'd creep down to hide your face behind a mask,
then joke with a batter.
He never knew it was you
who fed on his jibes and taunts
with that porous root, your face,
that you saved
everything fragile and fine,
unbinding of the cosmos,
how she was the dip and whorl in every ball
gathered behind the plate.

Yogi, somewhere beyond your closed eyes
and the trinket of time
all truth is compressed,

each crag and crevice
of your face is blessed,
as you whisper how, at bat,
your every home run had its heart in her,
how your every swing was you flinging on a rope
toward some beautiful idea, undefined,
until she in bright scarves
of love came swinging back,
Infinity's sweet curves
adorning her, turning your head
as it did your heart,
you saving a part in you
that danced there
in her pretty toes
dressed in the dust of this world.

When That Spiral at the Finish

flung back like wormy apples
Mick's home runs, making him grin,
it was Richardson,
the little second sacker,
he summoned to Dallas
to carry him as much as a mortal can
toward the seam.

It was not his drinking buddies,
Bauer and Skowron, venerable Yankees we still smell
in our mitt, who, try as they did
could not draw him through
the old stories to touch
yesterday's smooth face.
The passkey was a younger skin,
a boyish grin back in the 50's
when we chewed spirit gum.

It was Richardson he asked for—
a different version of him—
portly, fat on the Word,
who showed up to do
the unspeakable, dirty thing.
Leaning over, Richardson whispered
the holy river into Mickey's veins.

Mickey renounced once again
that worship he
could never slough off.

The burden of bearing up
this world he heaved upward.

Then Mick felt the oil of
Jesus' name release him,
more than his old barstools
fooled ceilings, more than his
sweet swing, now slow-
wheeling and small,
singing the green stirrings
of a perfect heart,
his own heart tripping
a slipped step
off the ladder of his bones.

Who's on First

toward the end of your career
when dribblers roll through?
It's not you, Lou Gehrig.
Your play, at the finish,
would be clean as your life.

Maybe there was no ball at all,
but someone laughing hard,
rolling through the aisles
between the legs of Costello. Or maybe
Gus Kahn was on piano,
backing up Abbott as he sings
with vehemence, "It Had to be Who,"
everything off key,
while in Ruth's scrubbed shadow,
your hat cocks back as if the brim
had nothing in your
blue eyes to hide.

Your life was clean as that white ball
growing magically
out of the dark sleeve of the umpire,
so that after games at Yankee Stadium,
you played broom ball
with the neighborhood kids, sweeping
them just short of highmindedness,
still able to
leave their rooms a mess.

Yes, What's Wrong is at first.
No, What is at second,
wearing Costello's jersey
with the huge P.U.,
as if they outdo the pigeons
who adorn the facade.
Who is on first.
And whose teammates are they
that loosen up and stretch,
knowing nothing but that you, Lou,
are not so lucky,
though you insist you are?
Is it Who that is speaking?

What is on second.
Who's on third? I Don't Know.
Then Abbott pushes the pie-faced Costello
into the face of Eternity, the manager,
who has a dazed look,
and is scratching his head,
leaving I Don't Know
to bear the questions
about your slump that dumped gravity,
until your mark on the world
was so light that you popped
a question over the head of Why,
the left fielder,
who's yet to comprehend it
in the web of his mitt.

When It is Over
God Slips a Finger into the Middle
of Yankee Stadium

where the playing field had been
to wear it,
finally, as His ring,

then hurls
His toothless junkpitch, the earth,
out past Pluto—
and all that science
tamed into existence.

He will see
that pure pennant race
when Jimmy Key belittled all of batdom,

and Jim Abbott
for one game
presided over the clarity
of a stream.

Everything
God will consider—
from vendors
selling the moon by the slice
to the flicker of deer
through Mattingly's wrist
as he turns on a pitch
takes back his career.

He will see the sparrow hits
of Velarde and Leyritz—how they lit
fast and shadowless
as God revealed a glimpse
of how He resided
in that space between fielders.

In His Highest
He will glory in
Bernie Williams' glove,
which was natural as a birdnest.

Then, perfect as He is,
God will grow even greater
like a fish freed from the aquarium,
that small space our faith
allowed for Him,
as He sets down
        Yankee Stadium,
        His ring,

on the other side of the cutting knife
held by someone unseen,
where Babe and John Blanchard take turns

      whistling drives

that come alive in our skin,
grazing it with warm stitches of laughter
at the crack of the bat,

then turn to watch them climb new walls,
the ones that limit understanding,
while singing in our blood—

the calming voice that has always been,

but clearer now, as when
we become
heartbeats in God.

Notes

The following baseball players, managers, coaches, and owners play major and minor roles in *The Ripening of Pinstripes*.

Dates in parentheses give player's years of service to team represented in poem. (Owners, managers, and coaches do not have years of service listed in this manner.)

> KEY: * denotes a Yankee in book
>
>   ∞ denotes a player who has a central role in poem

* **Abbott, Jim** (1993–94): one-handed pitcher who taped a childhood vow to locker that he would pitch in Yankee Stadium; more than fulfilled promise when he tossed no-hitter there in '93.

* **Alou, Felipe** (1971–73): best known of three Dominican-born Alou brothers who played in majors in the '60s and '70s; now the manager of the Expos.

* **Arroyo, Louis** (1960–63): his nasty screwball stymied hitters in early '60s; came in games early to preserve wins for Ford, whose arm, it was believed, needed abundant rest; 15 wins and 29 saves in '61.

* **Bauer, Hank** (1948–59): ex-Marine, two Purple Hearts and two Bronze Stars in WWII; known for aggressive all-out hustle in outfield and on bases.

∞* **Baylor, Don** (1983–85): before becoming manager of Rockies, was power hitter with MVP to his credit; had penchant for being hit by pitches and slamming line drives down third-base line.

* **Bengough, Benny** (1923–30): best defensive catcher in league before he hurt his throwing arm; a favorite of Babe who'd play catch with him while warming up before games.

∞* **Berra, Yogi** (1946–63): outstanding hitter, especially dangerous with the game on the line; excellent pitch-caller who appeared in record 14 World Series as player; three-time AL MVP.

Black, Joe (1952–57): NL Rookie of the Year in '52; considered best relief pitcher in league that season when he posted a 15-4 record with 15 saves and 2.15 ERA.

* **Blanchard, John** (1955; '59–65): in '61 one of record six teammates to hit 20 or more home runs in season; said he'd rather have been "scrub" for Yanks, which he was, than starter for another team, which he likely could have been.

∞* **Bouton, Jim** (1962–68): "Bulldog," a battler who was big winner before sore arm plagued him; his tell-all book *Ball Four* is a classic, though it alienated him from many former teammates (including Mantle) and baseball establishment; also known for brief return to majors as Braves' reliever eight years after his Major League career was "finished."

* **Boyer, Clete** (1959–66): outstanding third baseman always in shadow of Brooks Robinson, the Oriole great, and Clete's brother Ken, a power-hitting third baseman for the Cards.

Brock, Lou (1964–79): an explosive offensive force and swift left fielder who owned most of baseball's stolen base records before Rickey Henderson came along.

Busch, Gussie: owner and chief executive of Anheuser-Busch; purchased the Cardinals in 1953.

Bush, Guy (1923–34): Cub starter who had seven seasons in his 17-year career in which he won a minimum of 15 games.

Campanella, Roy (1948–57): stellar player; one of game's most popular; a catcher with three .300 seasons at bat; in '53 lead NL with 162 RBI; car accident ended career.

* **Cerv, Bobby** (1951–56, '60, '61–62): never more than 115 at-bats in six seasons before being sent to K.C.; there, had two huge years with the stick, then was traded back to sit again on Yankee bench; picked by Angels in expansion draft, then returned to Yanks to serve a third time.

∞ **Chapman, Ray** (1912–20): before he was felled by Mays' fastball, the classy shortstop, at 29, was looking forward to retiring at the end of year; was .278 hitter in nine big-league seasons.

* **Combs, Earl** (1924–35): speedy leadoff man in Murderers' Row; until 1986, held Yankee record for hits in season with 231.

* **Cone, David** (1995–): one of game's premier pitchers and toughest competitors; came to Yanks toward end of '95 season; invaluable down the stretch.

Cooperstown: the town in upstate New York where the Baseball Hall of Fame is located; synonym for the Hall of Fame.

Cox, Billy (1948–54): scintillating glove-work at third; a .262 hitter in 11 seasons.

* **Dent, Bucky** (1977–82): despite average range this steady, sure-handed shortstop was Yankee regular for 6 years; World Series MVP in '78.

* **Dickey, Bill** (1928–46): stalwart Yankee catcher; excellent hitter and fine handler of pitchers; under Dickey's tutelage, Berra became superior backstop.

∞* **DiMaggio, Joe** (1936–51): The Great DiMaggio of *The Old Man and the Sea*; in his time the best-known athlete in America and greatest all-around player; aloof and very much the loner, he led the Yankees by example; married to Marilyn Monroe for several years.

∞* **Duren, Ryne** (1958–61): for a time the most effective relief pitcher in baseball; an alcoholic who would "take a drink or ten," according to Stengel; rehabilitated after career ended; now counsels alcohol and drug-abuse patients.

* **Durst, Cedric** (1927–30): reserve who played outfield and first base for the Yankees.

Erskine, Carl (1948–59): owned a big breaking curveball; in third game of '52 Fall Classic struck out 14 Yankees for Series record; pitched two no-hitters.

∞* **Ford, Whitey** (1950–67): crafty left-hander; Yankee stopper of his day; two ERA titles to his credit, also 32 straight shutout frames in World Series.

Flood, Curt (1958–69): lifetime .293 hitter who won seven consecutive Gold Gloves; best known for challenging baseball's reserve clause, which soon led to free agency for players.

Fox, Terry (1961–66): had 29-19 lifetime record with 3.00 ERA.

Furillo, Carl (1946–60): top NL outfielder, this Pennsylvania native was called "The Reading Rifle" for outstanding throwing arm; knocked in a multitude of runs despite limited power.

∞* **Gehrig, Lou** (1923–39): member of original Murderers' Row; his game-playing streak of 2,130 games ended after he was stricken with disease that bears his name; hit .340 and slammed 493 home runs in 19 big-league seasons.

* **Gordon, Joe** (1938–46): quality second baseman and unselfish at the plate; advanced runners and did the essential things that don't show up in the box score.

* **Gossage, Goose** (1978–83): the hard-throwing right-hander was most intimidating pitcher in game when he arrived from the Pirates for the '78 season; lived up to expectations when he posted 27 saves and a 2.01 ERA.

* **Guidry, Ron** (1975–88): late blooming southpaw called "Louisiana Lightning" had formidable career; surreal season in '78 when he went 25-3 to help his team to second successive championship.

∞* **Henderson, Rickey** (1985–89): considered by many the game's best leadoff hitter of the '80s; controversial player who owns all-time stolen base marks but criticized for putting personal numbers ahead of his team; Billy Martin favorite in New York and in Oakland.

* **Henrich, Tommy** (1937–50): "Old Reliable"; plucky outfielder played key role at onset of '49 pennant race when he kept Yanks in hunt while DiMaggio suffered a bad heel.

Hodges, Gil (1943–61): big Dodger first baseman; one of best players never inducted into Cooperstown; managed 1969 Miracle Mets.

Hough, Charlie (1970–95): a knuckleballer who, at age 45, not only pitched but headed the Florida Marlins' rotation.

∞* **Howard, Elston** (1955-67): first black Yankee; very good player who lost some prime years by being in Berra's shadow; won MVP with .348 average in '61.

 * **Hoyt, Waite** (1921-30): outstanding right-hander for the Yankees; intelligent player later widely respected as radio announcer and storyteller; coined phrase, "It's great to be young and be a Yankee."

∞* **Jackson, Reggie** (1977-81): "Mr. October" for World Series heroics; slugged 563 career home runs; one of most exciting hitters, whether blasting a home run or striking out.

 * **Johnson, Cliff** (1977-79): 6'4", 225-pound catcher and first baseman; effective pinch hitter for Yankees; known for stepping out of box, taking worlds of time between pitches, when game was on the line.

 * **Keller, Charlie** (1939-49, '52): "King Kong"; outfielder and solid performer day in and out; his best was often saved for World Series; with DiMaggio and Henrich comprised what some believed to be the best Yankee outfield ever.

   Keltner, Ken (1937-49): through hard work became stand-out third baseman of the AL; seven-time All Star, had great throwing arm and wide range to his right; 163 home runs with .276 average over 13 seasons.

∞* **Key, Jimmy** (1993-96): stylish left-hander who pitches to the corners and keeps batters off stride; unpublicized yet one of the better pitchers in the game; signed with Orioles for '97.

   Killebrew, Harmon (1954-74): slugger with incredible power; 573 home runs in his Hall of Fame career.

 * **Kubek, Tony** (1957-65): graceful athlete and splendid shortstop with whom all who followed were compared for next thirty years.

   Labine, Clem (1950-60): fine Dodger left-hander; star reliever whose bread-and-butter pitch was an amazing sinking curve; retired Musial forty-nine consecutive times.

∞* **Larsen, Don** (1955-59): mediocre pitcher; for one game reached pinnacle when he fired no-hitter in Series; this one historic feat likely extended career to fourteen years when others with his record and talent would have been considered washed-up.

Lasorda, Tommy: the Hall of Fame Los Angeles manager who's said to bleed Dodger blue; known for inspirational style of managing.

* **Lazzeri, Tony** (1926–37): power-hitting second baseman with quick reflexes at bat and in the field; intelligent, soft-spoken and favorite of fans, especially Italian community.

* **Leyritz, Jim** (1990–1996): despite hot dog reputation, a valuable role player whose dramatics in post-season ('95 and '96) will keep him known in New York; signed on with Angels for '97.

∞* **Maas, Kevin** (1990–94): as rookie was Mattingly's replacement during injury-laden season; set Major League record for hitting his first 15 home runs in fewest at-bats (133); disappeared from the majors after several lackluster seasons in which his playing time was reduced; as recently as 1996 was invited to spring training by Yanks.

∞* **Mantle, Mickey** (1951–68): idol of almost every school lad in '50s and '60s; injuries and hard living cut short his career; in later years both legs wrapped before games while each at-bat was preceded by a roar; AL MVP in '56, '57 and '62.

∞* **Maris, Roger** (1960–66): left-handed pull hitter who broke Ruth's single-season home run record; was all-around player with good speed and Gold Glove in right field; consummate team player and MVP-winner in '60 and '61.

∞* **Martin, Billy** (1950–57): pugnacious, scrappy second baseman and clutch hitter in Fall Classic; as Yankee played above his ability; blamed for igniting brawl at the Copacabana, was devastated by trade to A's; his fiery and successful managing style brought him back to forefront of game.

∞* **Mattingly, Don** (1982–95): untouted when he first donned pinstripes; small for power hitter and slow afoot, but quick wrists at the plate, agility in the field plus vigorous work ethic made him the most dominant player of the '80s; back problems diminished his accomplishments and made him look human in second half of career.

∞* **Mays, Carl** (1919–23): only pitcher in majors to kill a batter with a pitch; shrewdness and a cold countenance made him disliked by even his teammates. The death pitch, a purpose pitch that got away, seemed to assure he'd not make the Hall despite being a top pitcher of his day and exonerated of blame in Chapman's death.

Mazeroski, Bill (1956–72): slick-fielding second baseman and Pirate mainstay for many years who, ironically, is best remembered for his big bat in '60 Series.

∞* **McDougald, Gil** (1951–1960): splendid infielder who performed admirably wherever Stengel needed him; a vital component of those great teams the Yankees fielded in the '50s.

* **Meusel, Bob** (1920–29): superb hitter with perhaps best throwing arm in baseball; a great athlete whose easy, fluid motions made him appear lackadaisical; miserly with words and those were seldom volunteered; his lack of endearment to the media, fans, and even teammates may have kept him out of Cooperstown.

Mitchell, Dale (1956): lifetime .312 hitter; more than ten seasons with Tribe when picked up by Dodgers to pinch hit in '56 pennant drive; at end of career was still an extremely dangerous hitter for Larsen to face for final out of perfect game.

* **Moore, Wilcy** (1927–29, '32–33): in his one great year, 1927, his record was 19-7, his sinker ball virtually unhittable.

∞* **Munson, Thurman** (1969–79): surly working-class catcher with tenacious nature and strong throwing arm; five times a .300 hitter; with Murcer was one of team's first legitimate stars in era that followed the demise of the team in mid '60s.

∞* **Murcer, Bobby** (1965–74, '79–83): heir-apparent to the Mick; never lived up but still very good player; in evening game following Munson's funeral, paid tribute to friend by almost single-handedly beating the Orioles in a stirring come-from-behind victory.

Murderers' Row: nickname for top of the 1927 Yankees batting order, which included Ruth, Gehrig, Combs, Lazerri and Meusel.

* **Nettles, Graig** (1973–83): power hitter who performed superbly at the hot corner; known for diving plays; showcased talents in Fall Classic, especially against Dodgers in '81.

∞* **O'Neill, Paul** (1993–   ): AL batting champion in strike-shortened 1994 season; a fine outfielder with outstanding throwing arm.

∞* **Pagliarulo, Mike** (1984–89): hard-nosed third baseman with work ethic that rivaled teammate Mattingly's; streaky hitter with power before injuries diminished output and he was traded; learned to go with the pitch; helped Twins to flag in '91.

* **Pasqua, Dan** (1985–87): muscular outfielder; part of influx of young home-grown players to team in mid '80's; 16 home runs and .291 average in 280 at-bats in '86 made him look promising.

* **Pennock, Herb** (1923–33): lanky pitcher whose great control and knowledge of opposing hitters was key to his success; the antithesis of his close friend, Ruth, by being regal in demeanor, eloquent, and intellectual.

* **Pepitone, Joe** (1962–69): perhaps peerless in raw talent; never lived up to hype of being next DiMaggio; became the bad boy instead who squandered his talents with poor work ethic and erratic behavior; in '88 served 6-month jail sentence for drug conviction.

* **Pipgras, George** (1923–33): primarily fastball pitcher; best season was '28 when he won 24 games for the Yanks.

Reese, Pee Wee (1940–58): graceful Dodger shortstop was in an elite class; also clutch hitter and considered by many the backbone of his team.

∞* **Richardson, Bobby** (1955–66): with Kubek was part of splendid double-play tandem; drove in 12 runs to set record in '60 Fall Classic; retired at age 32 to devote more time to God; established Baseball Chapel, a nondenominational ministry that organizes Sunday-morning chapels for all major-league teams and more than 160 minor-league teams.

* **Rivers, Mickey** (1976–79): speedster on bases and in Yankees'

cavernous center-field; weak throwing arm limited his value in the field; stole 43 bases in '76.

* **Rizzuto, Phil** (1941–56): pint-sized shortstop who won MVP in 1950 with .324 average; timely hitting and great defense took him to Cooperstown; popular Yankee announcer famous for his phrase "holy cow!"

Robinson, Jackie (1947–56): first black to break color barrier in majors; known for gritty competitive spirit, explosive speed and daring on the base path; Rookie of the Year in '47; MVP in '49.

Roe, Preacher (1948–54): beguiling left-handed spitball pitcher who twice led NL in won-lost percentage.

∞* **Ruth, Babe** (1920–34): "The Sultan of Swat"; arguably the game's greatest player and first bona fide power hitter; in first year with the Yanks he alone hit more home runs than any opposing team; would have made the Hall by virtue of pitching had he continued in that role (only two inducted pitchers have a better won-lost percentage).

∞ **Score, Herb** (1955–59): phenomenal young hurler whose career was shattered when hit in face by line drive; won 36 games and struck out 508 batters in two seasons.

* **Selkirk, George** (1934–42): "Twinkletoes"; strong right fielder; Yankee rookie at age 35; hit .300 five straight years.

* **Shawkey, Bob** (1915–27): right-handed pitcher; was Yanks first 20-game winner.

* **Showalter, Bucky**: coveted field boss for Yankees after years in farm system where he paid dues as player and manager; guided team to front of pack in disappointing strike-shortened season in '94, also to wildcard in '95.

* **Skowron, Bill** (1954–62): nicknamed "Moose"; steady performer who hit for both power and average during his tenure with the Yankees.

Smalley, Roy (1976–82, '85–87): good-hitting shortstop who clubbed 163 homers in a 13-year career.

Smith, Al (1953–57, '64): jack-of-all-trades in his years with Cleveland.

Snider, Duke (1947–62): sensational hitter known for strong arm in center; quick and graceful; for career blasted 407 homers, hit .300 seven times.

Stallard, Tracy (1960–62): Boston right-hander played seven seasons; 30-57 lifetime record attributed to his time with Mets when he was a 20-game loser despite a 3.78 ERA.

∞* **Stankiewicz, Andy** (1992–93): unheralded 27-year-old rookie exceeded all expectations when he filled in at shortstop at onset of '92 campaign; tired in second half and his average plummeted.

* **Steinbrenner, George:** controversial owner for whom the Yanks have won three World Championships.

* **Stengel, Casey:** colorful manager of Yankees who took team to postseason play ten times in twelve seasons.

Stobbs, Chuck (1953–58; '59–64): Senator pitcher who both started and relieved during his fifteen-year career; lifetime record was 107-130 with 19 saves.

* **Sturm, Johnny** (1941): 25-year-old first baseman whose injury during WWII ended career; in only season in majors hit .239 with 3 home runs and 36 RBI's in 524 at-bats.

* **Terry, Ralph** (1956–57; '59–64): despite serving up Mazeroski's famous home run in seventh game of '60 World Series, remained undaunted with 16-3 record in '61 and MVP award for the '62 World Series.

* **Torborg, Jeff:** fine defensive backstop who hit but .214 in majors; as coach and manager, known for innovative ideas and positive relationships with players.

* **Tresh, Tom** (1961–69): excellent shortstop, outfielder, and impact player; injuries robbed his career of some of its lustre; lifetime stats do not reflect vitality with which he played for several seasons.

* Velarde, **Randy** (1987–95): versatile sub adept in field and good with bat; helped Yanks to post-season in '95.

* White, **Roy** (1965–79): soft-spoken and classy; good hitter noted for speed and fine defense; graced pinstripes during lean years but stuck around to contribute to World Championships in late '70s.

∞* Whitson, **Ed** (1985–86): after big contract and huge expectations, was treated mercilessly by New York fans when he went 1-6 with a 6.37 ERA in first 11 starts in '85.

* Williams, **Bernie** (1991–): touted as coming superstar in minors; with each year of maturity, this gifted center fielder realizes more of his talent; a great postseason in '96 has begun to make his name known.

∞* Winfield, **Dave** (1981–90): graceful 6'6" outfielder who wielded a big bat; won numerous Gold Gloves and contributed greatly wherever he played; acrimonious relationship with Steinbrenner clouded his seasons in New York.

* Wynegar, **Butch** (1982–86): fine catcher in his years with Twins; suffered emotional turmoil after coming to Yanks, then had to catch Neikro brothers' notorious floaters.

Yastrzemski, **Carl** (1961–83): great all-around player whose unforgettable Triple Crown season was 1967 when he slugged 44 home runs, knocked in 121 runs and batted .326.

* Zimmer, **Don**: tenacious overachiever as player; again a Yankee coach, this time under Joe Torre, for whom he is a trusted advisor; has great baseball instincts, plays hunches with the best of them.

Rodney Torreson received an MFA in Creative Writing from Western
Michigan University. His poems have appeared in a wide range of jour-
nals and anthologies, including *The Third Coast, Passages North,* and
Hummers, Knucklers, and Slow Curves. He lives and teaches in Grand
Rapids, Michigan.

Author photograph © Mikel Cahill